Yes, I Can!

Written by Irma Singer
Illustrated by Michele Noiset

I can dance with a duck.

I can march with a moose.

I can sing with a seal.

I can giggle with a goose.

I can talk with a turtle.

I can bake with a bunny.

Yes, I can!

And I think it's all funny.